NLP

Acquire Expertise In The Skill Of Deciphering Individuals, Influencing Behaviour, And Exerting Mental Dominance. Explore The Many Strategies Of Influence And Observe How They Might Empower You To Resist Manipulation

Nikolaus Kasper

TABLE OF CONTNET

Can Giving Yourself Enough Time Help You Learn And Remember Things Better? 1

Easy Mind Control Methods To Apply 18

Nlp And Your Mental State 36

Remain Composed And Make An Effort To Bring Out The Best In Them. 55

Dark Psychology Techniques That Are Frequently Employed 72

Recognize That Not Every Choice You Make Will Work Out Well For You. 104

Creating A Viable New Belief 129

Can Giving Yourself Enough Time Help You Learn And Remember Things Better?

The majority of what is observed is continuously recorded by the unconscious brain. The subconscious is not there in the brain when you struggle with memory. Because there isn't a bridge between the two areas of the mind necessary for memory access, the characteristic makes amnesia more common. Setting aside some time to engage in activities like puzzles is essential since it improves a person's capacity for learning. These games and activities are vital since they facilitate better brain function. Exercising in your hectic schedule is essential to keeping your mind engaged. Thinking about and incorporating these activities into your daily routine is crucial. It is important to realize that you won't experience any difficulties with memory once the conscious and subconscious minds are in harmony. It is important to remember that studying and developing your ideas are vital processes providing you with knowledge and abilities essential for success in life. As a result, you must put in a lot of effort and develop your conscious minds to the point where they can comprehend concepts and store them securely for memory.

Chapter: A 21-Day Calendar

Everybody aspires to have or live a particular type of life that is more distinctive and professional. We all want to form certain essential habits to help us throughout our lives. The design may be licensed or more privately owned. However, forming these habits might be difficult sometimes, and if you don't schedule it, the desire might remain a nightmare. It's important to remember that committing to something for an extended period might develop into a habit worth listing. But not every practice is advantageous. Since it has been shown that negative habits can be established in as little as two days, the majority of these study papers concentrate on positive practices. It takes at least 21 days for those who sincerely want to form positive habits for the patterns to become ingrained in their lives.

The Basis of the Chronology

As previously mentioned, it might take up to 21 days to form a certain character—or, more accurately, habit. If someone wants to give up smoking, for example, it will take them at least 21 days to change and adopt a non-smoking lifestyle. The timeline was derived from Dr. Maxwell's interpretation, which stated that a person's unique self-image takes at least 21 days to form in person. On the other hand, many academics contend that his research was misconstrued and that it would take longer for a habit to change. Because of this, the 21-day pattern-forming myth has been branded. Many people use it to mold themselves or others into the person they want to be. To dispel this fallacy, researchers have been attempting to determine how long it takes to form a given habit. In actuality, though, it is feasible to establish a new practice in less than 21 days. It becomes a three-week span. Try as you can; doing something for the period may seem like an eternity, even though it sounds like a short time. For example, very few of us enjoy getting up early in the morning, particularly if we have nothing planned. It could also be challenging to form the habit of rising early if the weather is chilly and there is a lot of dew in the morning.

A particular habit must be developed consistently. It is important to remember that patterns make up 40–45% of our everyday actions and are just reinforced behaviors that become automated due to repetition. Automaticity plays a crucial role in the establishment of habits. Put another way, mastering the skill of consistency is essential if one wishes to form a specific habit. For example, it cannot be automatic to develop a strategy of rising early in the morning. For it to stick, waking up must be done consistently for a while. Being constant has the power to improve life and change people's perspectives. Put another way, each person develops their mental image, and getting out of bed becomes a ritual.

It is important to remember that routine or habit-building cannot be greatly accomplished without a strategic strategy. A plan is essential because it makes it possible to prepare the middle and implant the condition in the brain's subconscious. Thus, the mind prepares the body for the new habit, and following a time of conscious practice, the habit grows and integrates into the person. Put another way, following preparation, the body actualizes what the mind has envisioned and produces the intended result. The way the account is set up assumes a certain behavior after being exposed to a certain sort of life regularly, leading to change.

The replacement is another crucial element in the formation of a habit. To put it another way, the current activity must stop and be replaced by a new venture following the new pattern. For example, some actions or bad deeds result in this situation if one has been waking up late. Therefore, to form the habit of waking up, the person must tolerate certain activities and embrace others that will guarantee that they awaken on schedule.

The habit becomes fulfilling when one strives for achievement and gets rid of things that take away from the reward.

For example, if you have a habit of rising late, there's a good possibility you'll be late for your responsibilities and never have time to take care of your soul. It's also possible that viewing movies at night or conversing with pals keeps you up late. To get up early in the morning comfortably, you will need to give up on some of these hobbies. You should also create additional activities that will compel you to wake up and easily prepare for the day. Positive thinking is one thing that can assist one in achieving this. Such a critical perspective considers life's blessings rather than drawbacks. Such an attitude necessitates love, devotion, and endurance. You will be charged for and likely continue to undertake an activity if it benefits you. Thus, perseverance and dedication are needed to form this habit. Put differently, if an individual is determined to wake up for approximately 21 days, there's a possibility that this will also become a habit for them.

Deleted information is information that is omitted. The sender has intentionally, inadvertently, or presumptively stated something lacking in context, expecting the recipient to recognize and understand the implication. In the case above, I said, "He hates me," which is an example of a deletion. The pronoun and "unspecified noun" are introduced in place of the proper noun, or name, of the person being discussed, which is "deleted."

The "unspecified verb," which doesn't explicitly explain "how" the process is taking place, is another elimination. In addition, it could be applied allegorically and outside of its intended context. This one is a verb clause that isn't mentioned: "He's killing me with all these questions!" There are undoubtedly some deletions here. The "he" pronoun eliminates the proper noun that belongs. It is likely not being used in a literal sense when the word "killing" is used (ask the messenger to be sure), and NLPers are interested in knowing what specific questions to ask.

Additionally, the term "question" itself is a nominalization, which is the act of taking a verb or adverb and turning it into a tangible noun (or, to put it another way, the process of taking a verb and turning it into a concrete identity), therefore, when one asks, "Really! What did the questions look like? Were they threatening you directly, brandishing their weapons? By now, you should know how language can be changed, perverted, eliminated, nominalized, and misrepresented—all of which can confuse you!

Coincidentally, the nominalization "question" is derived from the verb "to ask," which is an action and is then transformed into the static word that we have come to know as "question."

The nominalization "relationship," which means "to relate," is one of my favorite ones to use as an example. If I were to tell you, "My wife and I get along great," Your mental model of the world—your experiences and past—allows you to interpret that in a way that makes sense to you. Thus, something is still lacking even if I denominalize the term "relationship" back to its verb form. Saying, "I relate well with my wife," for instance, What's absent? This still doesn't explain how well my wife and I get along, does it? What then remains to be found? The verb that isn't defined is missing. I may add, "I relate well with my wife's love of animals," for instance. We can go even further by repeating, "I relate well to my wife's love of cats," once we have become more detailed. The message gets clearer and more accurate the more particular a generic remark gets. We refer to this as chunking down information in NLP.

This is critical to understand because, even though you may be working in a group to generate ideas and conclusions about how to proceed with a specific project, upon reconvening, you may discover that much of what you had expected to be accomplished has not been completed in the manner you had thought. Because of this, you should be quite clear in your questioning and information sharing. Based on your communication model, just because you believe that you have disclosed what you intended to disclose doesn't mean the other person has understood your message as you intended.

As NLPers, we aim to eliminate the confusion (which is also a nominalization, incidentally!).

Another way to eliminate information necessary for total communication clarity is through comparisons. Saying, "I am doing much better now than I was, and I'm much happier too," is an example of a comparison. In this instance, "something" and "something now" are being compared using the adjective "better," but what? We can infer what the message could have meant based on prior experiences, but whatever conclusion we draw will represent the meaning received.

An additional component of deletion instances is judgments. Here's an illustration of what I mean: "You better get ready because God is returning soon!" Although the messenger is passing judgment, it is presented as an unquestionable fact. The NLPer may inquire, "Which god specifically will be coming?" for example. "Where precisely is that god going to be coming to?" "How will that god be making his appearance?" "What am I ready for?" "In what specific way are you ready?" "Why am I required to be prepared?" "What do you mean exactly when you say, "Ready"?" "When did God disappear?" "What day and precisely at what time is God coming?" "Soon, in contrast to what?" "How are you aware that God is coming?" And folks, this can go on and on and on, especially in light of the responses you get. By raising awareness and synthesizing communication, these questions can improve communicators' ability to connect with their audience more precisely and consistently.

Easy Mind Control Methods To Apply

We'll look at some of the manipulation strategies you can employ on your target, but first, let's talk about some of the approaches you can employ to the concept of mind control. A more severe kind of manipulation is called mind control, in which the manipulator attempts to take total control of the target's ideas, behaviors, and feelings in addition to influencing their decisions and thoughts.

In this chapter, we will discuss some of the true mind control methods traditionally employed in groups and by regular people in interpersonal relationships. Knowing how these operate can help you avoid being manipulated or use them to your advantage if you need to exert influence over someone. Among the most popular mind-control methods that are available are the following:

Separation

Isolation is the first mind control tactic that can be applied. People are highly gregarious animals. They enjoy conversing with people, going out in public, hanging out with their close friends and family, and engaging in more social activities.

People's perspectives on life can shift when we remove their social component.

Total physical seclusion may be the most effective. At this point, the subject is cut off from all forms of communication with people, including phone conversations, emails, social media posts, and in-person meetings. This has been observed in various groups, including cults. They will frequently transport the victim far from other people, leaving them with little human interaction except for their captors.

Now, achieving complete physical isolation can be difficult, and it is typically reserved for really dire circumstances. When attempting to manipulate someone, you generally don't want to go through and isolate the target. Still, it's customary for a manipulator to make every mental effort to reach their aim.

The manipulator might utilize various techniques to achieve their goals through manipulation. A week-long seminar in the country that keeps the individual away from their normal activities could be included. To make the target feel awful and make them quit visiting them, there could be a lot of remarks directed towards the person's close friends and family. Envy can be why the manipulator confines the target to their house and restricts the impact of outsiders on them.

The manipulator can provide information, withhold information, and take any other action they see fit to maintain as much influence over the target as they desire after they have control over the information sent to them. The manipulator can work and obtain what they desire from the target by making the objective dependent on them. The target is further trapped because no external cues alert them to a problem or warn them to be cautious.

Social Proof and Peer Pressure

Everyone enjoys having a sense of belonging to a group. Some people's main concern is fitting in; they will stop at nothing to be the life of the party, to win others over, and much more. Additionally, introverts prefer to spend more time at home than going out, partying, and socializing because they want to be sure that they fit in and are liked by others.

A manipulator may try to employ peer pressure and social proof against you. They are aware of your triggers when it comes to blending in and making friends. They will persuade their target to act in a certain way because it is the greatest method to help them fit in or because other people do it. The target will likely consent to it and follow the manipulator's wishes, whether or not they are true.

Social proof and even some degree of peer pressure are usually used by individuals who wish to control a larger population, such as those who want to persuade others to donate to their cause, to brainwash the newcomers. You'll discover that social proof is a phenomenon in which certain people believe that the opinions and behaviors of others are acceptable. They reason that if everyone else acts in a certain way, the consequences must also be legitimate.

It often doesn't matter what the other action is at all. This explains why, once they join a group, many people engage in activities that would not be considered appropriate in society. This may be beneficial when the person is unsure what to believe, act, or do. When people find themselves in these situations, they will observe what those around them are doing and decide to follow suit, regardless of the acts involved.

This is advantageous to the manipulator. Suppose they locate a new target to work with. In that case, they will have to either persuade the target that everyone else is participating in the activity or implement them into a group of others who the same individual has duped. The only ways the manipulator can increase the target's likelihood of getting what they want are by employing social proof and, if others are involved, some peer pressure.

Remarks

Although criticism is sometimes employed in isolation, it can also be utilized independently. Criticism can make the other person feel insecure and like they are doing something wrong, so manipulators like to use it. The objection can be directed at any number of things, including the person's views, friends, appearance, or even the clothes they wear.

When a manipulator tries to use criticism to their advantage, they frequently want to cover it up with a compliment or softball critique that ends with a jab. This lets them exploit the critique, but if their target becomes upset, they can always turn the argument around and say their target is simply being sensitive or mishearing them.

The critique will typically begin very mildly. Since no one enjoys criticism, the manipulator won't want to start with a large issue since, if you start with a big issue, the target would just flee and stop being near you. The manipulator is skilled at making mildly painful remarks and can sow a small, hardly perceptible seed of self-doubt.

Something like, "I didn't know that green is your color," could be their opening statement. I believe you ought to throw it out. This one makes fun of the target's clothing and claims you don't look nice in that color. When you wear your favorite clothing or dress up for a night out, they might even decide to say anything along these lines. Even though what they said wasn't very hurtful, the exchange's tone and circumstances were enough to make the person start to doubt themselves.

With time, the manipulator will begin to point out more and more flaws in the person they are targeting to increase their self-doubt. Because they begin to believe that they are unlikable and have several defects, the target may become increasingly dependent on the manipulator. Because people perceive the manipulator's continued presence as an indication of their concern, they will begin to comply with the manipulator's requests more and more.

To increase their chances of asserting their dominance, the manipulator can decide to criticize the outside world. The manipulator says you ought to be overjoyed that they would want to be associated with you. They present themselves as significant to persuade you that they are necessary, and you ought to be delighted that they desire to spend time with you.

Speed is another crucial component of spoken communication. Since some people are naturally rapid talkers and others are naturally slow talkers, this is one of the trickiest parts of speech. Then there are people who talk very quickly when they're anxious, and there are those who go into lockdown when they're anxious. For this reason, it's critical to be aware of your speaking pace.

For instance, it would be ideal to talk clearly and slowly if you were giving an educational speech. This is because you want to ensure you don't overestimate yourself. Indeed, most people think more quickly than they can say. As a result, the brain functions more quickly than the mouth. This could lead to a conflict between all the moving components involved in speaking. As such, it's simple to become stuck in your speech.

You may make sure that others will think you are in charge of what you have to say by keeping a steady cadence. Speaking too quickly will make people assume you're frightened, and they might even ignore you completely. Speaking too slowly can give the impression that you are patronizing others. If that's the case, you might irritate a few folks. Naturally, you might wish to talk more slowly if you are addressing a group of people whose primary language is not English.

Aiming for 8 to 10 syllables for each breath is a good guideline. You can feel short of breath if you speak more than ten words. It may appear you are hyperventilating if you breathe in too quickly. Therefore, maintaining a steady cadence will undoubtedly make you appear composed and in charge.

Thus, you may be staring at someone tense and/or nervous if you listen to them talk very quickly. This could be a blatant indication that the speaker is not proficient in the subject. Maybe they are, but they're just uncomfortable right now. In either case, this can help you understand this person's mental state during the conversation.

This chapter's last point has to do with stress. We are not discussing the tension that comes from having too much job to do. Here, the inflections applied to particular words and phrases are called stress. For example, "opportunity" is how the word "opportunity" is pronounced. The stressed syllable in the word is indicated by the capital letters

"TU." This is crucial for all languages because mispronounced syllables can make communicating difficult. At most, the listener would just hear a strange word.

Furthermore, a sentence's meaning can be drastically changed by changing the emphasis on various terms. Let's examine an illustration.

Let's say you are discussing a stolen object. In defense of themselves, the accused claims, "I didn't do it."

The italicized version of the word "I" signifies that the word was stressed in the statement. Thus, the accused argues that, although the action happened, they were not accountable. The defendant may reply, "I didn't do it."

In this instance, the accused is stressing that they did nothing. All they are doing is denying that they stole the object.

Consider this possibility now.

It was not me.

The accused implies that they did not perform the conduct by emphasizing "do." They might have done something different, but not that. Maybe the person who is being accused is just trying to say that they have nothing to do with what happened.

In the preceding instance, the defendant merely wishes to highlight that they bear no responsibility for the deed that has been done. But what if the sentence's meaning could be entirely altered by merely moving the point of emphasis?

Think about this scenario:

I cherish you.

This is an expression of how you feel.

I cherish you.

You say that only you and no one else adore you when you emphasize the pronoun "I."

I cherish you.

The verb "love" is stressed in this instance. This indicates that it is not just another activity but love.

I cherish you.

Lastly, putting a lot of emphasis on "you" indicates that just "you" is the object of my devotion.

In this instance, it is evident that you are referring to distinct parts of the same sentence by shifting the location of the stress. So please remember that you can make your argument very obvious by toying with stress. It can also be utilized to produce an impact. In light of this, stress can be useful for efficient communication.

NlpAnd Your Mental State

The basic idea behind neuro-linguistic programming is the application of NLP to effect change. And is there a more profound inside shift than a mental shift? The word "state" is frequently used in NLP. This is a reference to your emotional and mental health. This is a reference to your emotional and mental health.

The majority of people will experience a range of mental states even though their mental state and their self-concept may be irrevocably linked. These emotions include complacency, anger, sorrow, or pleasure. You can alter your mental state with the use of NLP. By altering the language in your brain, this is accomplished. NLP can assist you in overcoming negative emotions, low self-esteem, or depression.

Use a visualization comparable to the one you employed to boost your self-worth. Consider your description of the day. Now, visualize clearing your mind of all unfavorable ideas. Speaking to yourself positively can boost your self-esteem. Imagine yourself in a cheerful, peaceful, or loving situation, perhaps with a loved one. What words of comfort would they offer you?

Your perspective mostly determines your mental state. Your emotional state is determined by how you perceive the environment around you. To enhance your mental well-being, NLP can assist you in altering your views and convictions. When you can modify your opinion, having a positive self-concept and leading a happier life is simpler.

Now, let's examine how NLP might enhance your self-perception and how self-perception affects your ability to connect and interact with people.

LINKING UP WITH OTHERS

NEURO-LINGUISTIC PROGRAMMING has numerous applications in fostering interpersonal connections and is a very helpful technique for enhancing self-awareness. This is a crucial component. It facilitates the identification of your communication style. This has a direct bearing on your character. Some are more gregarious and have no trouble conversing with total strangers. Some are less outgoing and think they aren't good at striking up conversations.

How you communicate might be greatly influenced by your perception of yourself. The relationship between self-concept, communication style, and NLP will be discussed in this chapter. Additionally, you'll discover how to apply NLP to enhance communication.

Applying NLP to Improve Communication

You can enhance your communication abilities with the help of neuro-linguistic programming. NLP can help you learn how to control your emotions, handle uncomfortable social situations, express your ideas, and set boundaries constructively and successfully.

You can apply the modeling and visualization tools you've learned to improve your listening, speaking, and emotional conveying skills to meet your communication goals. You will also study anchoring after studying NLP techniques to strengthen or enhance communication. By associating feelings and images with your emotions, you can instantly recall them. Now, let's get going! First, let's talk about visualization. If you find it difficult to communicate effectively, you should learn to be more aggressive. What if you don't think well of yourself or are shy? Examining why you are a poor communicator is critical, and being honest with yourself is critical. Visualization can help you become a more confident and effective communicator if you have a clear purpose. You'll need to apply the visualization skills that helped you enhance your self-concept. These activities aim to improve your confidence and sense of self. You will need to generate imagery to assist you in seeing yourself in a challenging circumstance. Perhaps you find it difficult to communicate with a coworker. Maybe they're hostile or frightening.

To begin with, picture yourself interacting with your coworker in your typical manner. Maybe you avoid talking to your coworkers or allow them to take advantage of you. Picture yourself confronting a coworker. Pay attention to the words you use. Consider your feelings regarding the language. Picture yourself getting up straighter and taller. After you have finished visualizing:

Keep the mental image in mind.

Think back to that picture the next time you work with this coworker. You'll be amazing at anchoring this experience.

Remain firm, polite, and forceful; don't allow your supervisor or coworker to take advantage of you.

It will get easier to speak up once you've done it a few times. Your colleague will likely back off and follow your lead.

You can gain control and confidence by modeling. Think of someone whose confidence you appreciate. You can utilize the modeling skills covered in Chapter 3 to mimic their communication style. Respect is given to confident people by their deeds and interactions with others; they do not demand it. You can observe the conduct of someone you admire in their assertive communication abilities by getting to know them.

When assessing the communication skills of another person, pay attention to what they say and watch how they behave. Communication that is both verbal and nonverbal frequently overlaps. You can effortlessly incorporate every facet of successful communication techniques as a forceful communicator. As we've already established, forceful communicators also make great listeners. You must develop your listening skills to increase your passive communication abilities.

Your NLP abilities can be used to imitate the desired behavior of the person you wish to be like. Consider how you would respond to a given circumstance. Then, picture them carrying out the same action. Put yourself in their position and role-play the situation. Now consider the language they would use and how they would use it. Once you are comfortable with the language, you can start reciting it.

When discussing language that exudes confidence, we mean eliminating any filler words or phrases that can imply hesitation or insecurity. If you are unsure about anything, state it as follows:

Summary: "I think that the client likes this setup."

"The client likes this setup," you say with assurance. Filler: The conference seems to have gone quite nicely.

Prospective Velocity

Future Pacing is an NLP technique in which the subject is guided to a future state, and possible future outcomes are practiced so that the desired outcome occurs automatically. This mental picture, or visualization technique, is utilized to visually experience and anchor a change or resources to future scenarios.

A competent manipulator may take their target on a mental trip into the future and shape how they react when it does. To eventually get their own desired outcome into the victim's psyche, a professional NLP user with prominent Dark Psychological qualities may cognitively transfer their victim into the future and offer outcomes while keeping an eye on the victim's reaction.

Impact and Convincing

This is by far the most ambiguous NLP approach, residing somewhere in the middle between psychotherapy and dark psychology.

While eradicating unpleasant emotions, breaking harmful habits, and resolving disputes are the main goals of NLP, ethically influencing and persuading people is another facet of the field. Now, notice that this instance uses the word ETHICAL.

Leading hypnotist and founder of the "American Society for Clinical Hypnosis," Milton Erickson, was one of the notable psychology therapists involved in Grinder's initial study on NLP. Because of his extraordinary skill at hypnosis, Erickson was able to converse with people's subconscious minds without the necessity for hypnosis and genuinely hypnotize anyone, anywhere.

He contributed to creating the NLP "Milton Model," which uses abstract linguistic patterns to put subjects in a trance-like condition. The Milton Model states that purposefully ambiguous and artistically imprecise sentences will cause the listener to infer the meaning of what they hear from their own experiences and fill in the details subliminally.

This effective method can help people overcome fears, deal with deep-seated negative emotions, and become more self-aware and ethically influencing and persuading others.

Using NLP to Deceive

You can see that NLP has a lot of power. It can persuade you to think of different ideas that will alter how you behave. But someone can do something similar to those around them when put in the wrong hands. These are easy ways for manipulators to manipulate you and influence your thinking. When you confront this, you find that, in the end, the user is the real issue, not the methods themselves. The act of manipulating others and having the ability to change their perceptions of you is not intrinsically harmful or immoral. Being able to change your own or other people's thoughts is not inherently problematic; the motives do matter, though.

Indeed, you could break someone down with NLP. You could try to undermine the confidence and self-worth that define them as individuals. You can come up with fresh ideas for them that transform how they approach everything. You may intentionally interact with others in damaging or cruel ways, or you could interact with them in a way that improves them. Consider this: How frequently do you witness experts purposefully modifying the minds of others? They take a different tack when dealing with individuals. Take a minute to consider therapists or even NLP practitioners. NLP was created to enable people to change their thoughts therapeutically. It is extremely powerful and effective since it was designed to bring about those changes. Ultimately, ensuring that you know better is the only approach to guarantee that you can perform better. To ensure you are not harming others, ensure you are conscious of your actions. If you choose to employ NLP, keep in mind your power. If you're concerned about being manipulated by others, recognize the influence that NLP has. With this understanding, periodically ask yourself if you are acting because you want to or only doing it because you feel compelled to. You will be more capable of defending yourself if you learn to distinguish between these subtleties. It will be possible for you to utilize NLP on your own to affect yourself as well, and doing so won't cause any issues.

When in doubt, it's best to consider the situation objectively, maintain your composure, and maintain a certain degree of detachment.

Do Others Easily Influence You?

There are many easy attributes for manipulators to take advantage of. Among other traits, manipulators specifically look for people who are inexperienced, overly trusting, impressionable, impulsive, in need of approval all the time, lack assertiveness, and are always trying to please others.

That suggests that concentrating on your personal growth is one of the simplest methods to avoid dishonest coworkers. The more confident you feel about yourself, the harder it is to control you and the less of them you engage with.

And there's health in the statistics. Begin to lean toward coworkers who are diligent, upbeat, and courteous. Even while you can't instantly improve your self-esteem, you can start making different connections with others tomorrow.

How to Handle Capable Coworkers

You may likely encounter dishonest supervisors at some point in your career, so it's good to learn how to maintain a constructive working relationship with them. Here are several ways to accomplish this:

1. Desire to observe things from their perspective.

Identifying the reasons behind dishonest colleagues' actions is the most effective technique to have a conversation with them.

The person is probably accustomed to acting this way and has witnessed it work. They could think that's the only way to get someone to pay attention to them.

Attempt to accept it rather than pass judgment on what they did. Understanding things from their perspective is the first step in forming a productive working relationship with these men.

Remain Composed And Make An Effort To Bring Out The Best In Them.

The best way to deal with dishonest behavior is to remain silent, try to pick up on any subtleties that the person may have given away and be discrete.

Placing the blame on the person is the worst course of action since it will just motivate them to justify their actions further.

Since reality is rarely clear-cut, likely, this man isn't all that bad. When you focus on any of their more endearing qualities rather than their less appealing ones, it comes through in your interactions with them, making them more like you and less in need of bothering you.

3. Refrain from letting their behavior or feelings dictate how you feel or respond.

The worst thing you can do when dealing with dishonest supervisors is to allow them to control your emotions, although this is easier said than done.

Anyone who acts domineering, enraged, or obviously frustrated just serves to fan the flames.

It's more crucial to realize that while you can't control their actions, you can control how you respond to them. Remain composed and behave in a courteous, upbeat, and focused manner regardless of how close your coworkers are to things.

Never give up on them or try to make up for their actions with your own. Man, get over it.

4. Only take action when it benefits both parties; therefore, don't hesitate to decline requests.

Even though a misanthropic colleague may craft a proposal, the question must not be misleading. Their counsel may often prove beneficial.

It's best to keep an open mind and think things through before answering "yes" or "no" to a question. If the answer will hurt rather than help you, don't hesitate to say "no." One of the most important things when managing a coworker is assertiveness.

Experts in the art of persuasion, dark ones, will use gradualism to raise the intensity of their arguments gradually. They know that no victim would be inclined to commit a major crime or wrongdoing immediately or jump the canyon. To get there, the persuader works to create a bridge. It's too late for the victim to escape when they realize how far they've gone.

Hiding Up the Real Goals

A persuasive speaker might employ several dark psychology techniques to get their desired outcomes. They must mask their actual desires if they are to succeed. The most skilled persuaders can employ this strategy in several ways, but the strategy they select will frequently rely on the victim and the circumstances.

One tactic a persuasive speaker employs is the notion that many people will find it difficult to say no to two requests made in quick succession. Assume that the person who persuaded the victim to part with $200 does not intend to repay the money. The person trying to convince can start by stating that they require a $1,000 loan. They might elaborate on what would happen to them personally if the persuader cannot provide that amount of money shortly.

It is possible that the victim will feel remorse or sympathy for the persuader and wish to lend a hand, but $1000 is a large sum of money and more than the victim can lend. The persuader will now reduce their request from $1000 to $200, which is their desired initial amount. The victim has an emotional reason for requiring the money and cannot turn down this second request. They regret not complying with the first request when it was made and wish to support the persuader. The victim won't know what happened, and the persuader ends up with the $200 they initially desired.

Reverse psychology is a different kind of persuasion strategy that the advocate may employ. In persuasion, this can also aid in disguising genuine motives. A boomerang personality is attributed to certain individuals. This implies that they will veer off in different directions rather than follow the direction in which they are thrown.

If the persuader is acquainted with someone who leans more toward the boomerang style, they can pinpoint a major vulnerability in that individual. Let's take the scenario where a persuasive person's friend tries to get a female they like. The friend will utilize that girl and subsequently hurt her, the persuader knows. The girl is caught between an evil buddy and a trustworthy outsider. The person trying to convince her might attempt to point her toward the guy who is genuinely a wise decision, even though they know she would defy them and choose the dangerous friend instead.

Leading Inquiries

Leading questions are an additional technique for dark persuasion. If you've ever dealt with a knowledgeable salesperson, you know that verbal persuasion may have a significant influence when used with caution and nuance. Leading questions are among the most effective verbal communication strategies.

Any queries that elicit a particular reaction from the victim will qualify as leading questions. An inquiry along the lines of "How bad do you think those people are?" will be posed to the target by the persuader, implying that they are unquestionably bad to some degree. Instead, they may have used a non-leading query like, "How do you feel about those people?"

Leading inquiries is a skill that masters of the dark persuader use in a way that is difficult to detect. It will be difficult to guide or convince the victim if they ever start feeling like they are being led. A persuader will stop using that one and use another if they ever feel their victim is beginning to realize what is happening. They might use that strategy again, but only after the victim has calmed down and is more likely to be swayed.

State Transfer Law

The concept of state examines an individual's whole emotional condition. People are in a powerful and harmonious condition when they are in harmony with their words, ideas, and actions. According to the law of state transference, the individual in a position of power can project their emotional state onto the other person with whom they are communicating. The dark persuader can use this very effectively against their target.

The influencer will first try to push their state to coincide with the one their target naturally possesses. Should the target be depressed and speak slowly, the influencer will force their condition to conform to this pattern. Building a strong relationship with the target is the goal.

The influencer will then carefully change their state once we reach this state match to check whether they comply with the victim. Maybe they'll decide to speak more quickly to see whether the victim does the same. The influencer has reached the hook point when the victim exhibits these compliance signals.

The influencer would alter their state to the one they wish the victim to have as soon as this hook point is reached. However, depending on the target and circumstances, it might take some time. The influencer may be aiming for this particular emotional state. It could be angry, joyful, optimistic, or offended. Often, it relies on what the person trying to convince wants to accomplish. This is a crucial strategy for a dark persuader to adopt since it will demonstrate how subconscious cues affect the success or failure of persuasion in general.

Mood Variations and Irrational Conduct

Your lover is training you to submit to their will if they become upset or angry when you disagree with them or treat you like you're unworthy of their love for voicing an honest opinion. There is very little, if any, space for disagreement for the manipulator. Only the whole submission and agreement will be accepted.

Anything less will lead to unpredictable conduct and abnormal mood swings. Some manipulators have severe violent or aggressive outbursts. Because of sheer terror, the mere prospect of this outcome will persuade their victims to continue being submissive. Avoiding someone is a good idea if you notice abrupt and drastic shifts in their attitude or emotions, especially if there is no apparent cause or event for the change. This conduct will worsen and intensify with time, especially if you figure out their trick and have to break free from their manipulative hold.

Never Give Up

For mind control to be effective, total obedience is necessary. No more room for compromise or other ideas. All viewpoints are respected in a healthy relationship, even when they are divergent or involve particular subjects. It can persuade someone that they are unworthy or uncompromising if you don't allow them to voice their opinions without mockery or condemnation. It also qualifies as emotional and psychological abuse. When even the tiniest judgments or ideas are twisted to the manipulator's agenda, it is simpler to spot this warning sign. This can refer to anything from picking a movie to watch to a restaurant for supper, which influences wider choices like getting a mortgage or establishing a family. When it comes to potential long-term relationships, recognizing when someone is not willing to compromise can spare you a great deal of misery in the future.

Who Makes Use of Mind Control? Organizations, High-Level Committees, and Individuals We Know and Meet in Daily Life

Who and why use mind control techniques? Many people who are vulnerable to mind control often aren't even aware that they are. Different persons (individuals) and groups use mind and thought-control tactics for various reasons.

Knowing their goal also helps to explain why specific strategies are employed and how to spot them. We could unknowingly be subjected to covert manipulation or influence when we go about our daily lives—for example while driving to work or school, grocery shopping, or doing errands—by a sales pitch or billboard advertisement.

We would become aware of how frequently persuasion bombards our minds if we stopped every time we saw an advertisement, a promotion, or a person or representative trying to "pitch" a sale or solicit a donation. We will only pay attention to select advertisements or individuals; others will pass us by.

Section 6: Definition of Dark NLP

There are situations in which you might employ these dark psychology techniques without intending to deceive someone, even if some people will use them to hurt their victim. Some of these strategies were purposefully or inadvertently introduced to our toolkit through several channels, such as:

As a child, you observed the behavior of adults, particularly those in your immediate vicinity.

Your mind was expanded, and you could better comprehend the activities of others around you as an adolescent.

You got to see other people apply the strategies and ultimately be successful.

At first, you might have used the strategies accidentally, but as soon as you saw they effectively achieved your goals, you would start using them on purpose.

Certain individuals, such as public speakers, politicians, and salespeople, are trained to employ these strategies to achieve their goals.

Dark Psychology Techniques That Are Frequently Employed

Love flooding is when you flatter, praise, or show someone affection to persuade them to agree with your request. You can employ love flooding to make someone feel wonderful and increase the likelihood that they will assist you in moving certain stuff into your home. A cunning manipulator could also use it to elicit feelings of attachment from the other person and persuade them to take action against their better judgment.

Lying would be providing the victim with a false account of what happened. Exaggerations or a partial truth may also be used to accomplish your goals.

Love denial: This can be difficult for the victim since it can give them the impression that the manipulator has forgotten them. This is keeping love and affection from the victim until you can acquire what you want from them.

Withdrawal: This is the process by which the victim is ignored or treated silently until the other person's needs are met.

Limiting options: The manipulator may allow their victim to make some decisions, but this is done to divert attention away from the decisions they don't want the victim to make.

Semantic manipulation is a tactic where the manipulator uses widely understood words and has mutually agreed-upon meanings in a conversation. Later on, though, they will confess to the victim that their original meaning of the word was quite different. Even though the victim was duped, the new meaning frequently modifies the definition entirely and may cause the conversation to go as the manipulator intended.

Reverse psychology is giving someone instructions, knowing full well that they would act oppositely. However, the manipulator's original intention was for the opposite outcome.

Who Will Employ Dark Tactics on Purpose?

A wide range of individuals against you could employ these devious strategies. They can be encountered in various spheres of your life, so knowing how to avoid them is crucial. Those that are capable of purposefully employing some of these dark psychology techniques include:

Narcissists: They will need to convince others that they are better than them, and they will have an exaggerated sense of their value. They will employ dark psychology and persuasion to fulfill their desire to be revered and adored by everyone they encounter.

Sociopaths: Sociopaths are persuasive, clever, and endearing people. However, they only take these actions to achieve their goals. They are emotionless and incapable of feeling regret. This indicates that they have no problem employing strategies from dark psychology to achieve their goals, even going so far as to establish flimsy relationships.

Politicians: By persuading someone that their viewpoint is correct, a politician might use dark psychology to win someone around to their way of thinking.

Salespeople: Not every salesperson will employ devious methods to harm you. However, it's likely that some people—especially those who are genuinely focused on increasing their sales figures and dominating their competition—will use dark persuasion without a second thought.

Leaders: Many leaders throughout history have employed dark psychology tactics to influence followers, subordinates, and people to behave as they like.

Selfish people: These might be any individual you encounter who prioritizes their needs over those of others. They don't care about other people, and they'll let them give up their advantages so they may have their own. It doesn't matter if someone else gains from the circumstance if it helps them. However, if anyone is going to lose, it will be the other person, not them.

This list will have two uses, which makes it significant. It can aid in self-realization and make you more conscious of others attempting to coerce you into doing things against your choice. One of the main purposes of this guidebook is to equip you to fight dark psychology by helping you recognize those who are trying to take advantage of you and don't care about the consequences.

Gaining the Likes of Others (Rapport)

These are straightforward NLP techniques, yet they can help you get along with almost anyone. There are a ton of ways to build rapport with someone. NLP is the source of one of the most efficient and captivating methods. This tactic involves empathetically mirroring the words, tone of voice, and nonverbal cues of others.

People like other people who are similar to them. Unobtrusively reflecting the other person causes the mind to fire "reflect neurons," which are joy sensors in the cerebrum that give people a happy feeling when they mirror someone else.

The primary tactic is to either stand or sit in the same position as the other person. In the same manner, tilt your head. Smile when they smile. Resemble how they appear on the outside. When they cross theirs, fold yours. Repeat what they say, and so forth.

Nuance is how an unaware affinity is created. In the unlikely event that you are overly transparent, the other person might see you on purpose, which would probably ruin your compatibility. So keep your reflection regular and calm.

Influence and Convincing

While a significant portion of NLP is devoted to assisting people in eliminating unpleasant emotions, unfavorable habits, conflict, and the list goes on, another portion of NLP focuses on influencing and persuading others ethically.

Milton H. Erickson was one of the mentors in the field. Erickson was a therapist who also studied the subliminal mind using hypnosis (the real, coherent material, not the meaningless amusement trance you see in organized appearances).

Because Erickson was such a skilled spellbinder, he developed a method for dealing with people's subconscious personalities that didn't involve trance. He could genuinely captivate people in casual conversations at any time.

This is a fantastic tool that can be used to influence and persuade people, as well as to help people overcome obstacles, fear, training convictions, and more without conscious awareness. In the unlikely event that they knew, who would be safe in some way (think high school students who would prefer not to pay attention)?

Setting Up

Subordination is the setting of all significance. When a picture is displayed outside a handicraft exhibition, people's perceptions of it are altered. It transforms into "a gem". When Marcel Duchamp's "Wellspring," a mere porcelain urinal, was placed in a showcase case at a craftsmanship exhibition in 1917, it became a show-stopper. It ignited an uprising in craftsmanship.

Thus, to the extent that we can tell, the context in which something is presented affects its meaning. There aren't many publications currently discussing the common edges NLP has identified and how we can use them.

There are two methods for rephrasing ideas or justifications to persuade people to change their minds. These methods include either altering the context in which they see an event or the meaning they attribute to it.

Frequently Used NLP Frames

Here are some of the 'standard' diagrams commonly used in NLP and some ideas for possible applications.

Final Frame

The 'Result Frame' is related to evaluating situations about the ideal outcomes or goals you have established for yourself. These outcomes should be 'all around shaped' (according to the definition). The Outcome Frame provides a clear rationale for evaluating any action or occurrence: does it advance you toward your ideal outcome or move you away from it?

The Natural Frame

This is about how an event or action affects the larger frameworks of which we are a part, such as our family, group, association, network, or whole world. Does your suggested activity consider your and others' credibility as people? When you experience inconsistency in your thinking typically indicates that you must pay attention to your surroundings.

"As if" Frame

Using the 'As though' template, one might explore possible outcomes for creative critical thinking. For example, what would happen if a particular situation aspect differed?

Models:

"What might Richard Bandler do right now?"

"Where will we be a half year from now, and how could we arrive?"

"What's the most noticeably terrible thing that could occur, and how might we handle it?"

The 'As though' outline is the basis for organizing scientific possibilities and testing PC frameworks!

You can also use the 'As though' template to convince a group of people to view the situation as though they have just achieved the best outcome possible. Ask them to describe the outcome, what they will see, hear, and feel, its effects, etc. This will help them feel more and more motivated to take action and help them believe in the outcome.

Rewind Frame

The 'Backtrack Frame' is handy for meetings, discussions, and planning. To apply it, you would use the other person's watchwords and tonalities to summarize what they have stated. Checking for understanding and comprehension of previous statements promotes compatibility and is beneficial when new members join the group. When a group stalls out, it is also very beneficial to go back to the original goal of understanding so you can start over at the point before the discrepancy happens.

Meaningful Frame

This is an additional advantage that is useful at events. In the unlikely event that a group member speaks or behaves in an irrelevant way to the strategy or the desired outcome, asking, "How could that be significant?" can help get everyone back on track.

Distinctive Frame

The 'Difference Frame' can be employed in the following two or three ways:

If, while you consider your future path, you are going to gather inspiration or look into possible outcomes, you may weigh an ideal outcome against the situation as it stands or consider an alternative. This decides on more available choices and presents the outcome from a progressive perspective. The elements of the existing situation you choose to highlight and your choices to balance the desired outcome will affect the final appearance.

You can put your endorsed decision in a better light by balancing it with another decision when marketing or exerting influence. For example, if you point to the most costly item first, even if it's still really valuable, the next item will seem like a better deal. Accordingly, if you ask your colleagues to take action, it will be easier for them to comply if it is presented differently than something that is far more difficult and problematic.

Chapter 11: People to listen to and books to read

The field of neuro-linguistic programming is always changing. It has its leading representatives because of this. Reading the works of its pioneers, such as "The Structure of Magic I: A Book About Language and Therapy" " is definitely worthwhile if you want to learn more about neurological programming. Studying these authors' writings is undoubtedly useful because they developed the neuro-linguistic programming approach, the body of scientific information that allows us to learn more.

But if you're looking for a book that will give you a lot of motivation. They're written in an easy-to-read style and include numerous exercises, neuro-linguistic programming techniques, and plenty of inspiration and problem-solving recipes. These books serve as links to build better lives. It is also uncommon to come across materials that, when read again, provide satisfactory solutions to your queries. The books are presented in an easy-to-read style with lots of humor and educational anecdotes that inspire you to take action. Numerous assignments are available to consolidate recently obtained knowledge and its prompt application in real-world scenarios.

Throughout the world, Anthony Robbins is a highly regarded and well-known motivational speaker. Using techniques from neuro-linguistic programming and other approaches, he has facilitated numerous training sessions and motivational speeches and assisted many people. Many of his talks are accessible as coaching session recordings that have aided in the development of millions of individuals worldwide.

There will undoubtedly be a lot of NLP and method talk that you may use in your situation. This curriculum, which integrates coaching, neuro-linguistic programming, spirituality, and psychology, is unquestionably expanded. Tony Robbins frequently demonstrates in his coaching sessions how simple it is to make long-lasting, positive changes in yourself that positively impact relationships with others, the creation of a better future, and numerous other successes in various spheres of life. These changes simply help one become a better version of themselves—a happy, fulfilled individual who realizes all of their dreams.

Look over these books right away—the information they contain is invaluable! Try training programs on CDs and other learning resources, such as audiobooks, which you may listen to, for example, while operating a motor vehicle, if they are more applicable to audio-visual materials. You can always try the method right now by enrolling in coaching workshops or neuro-linguistic programming classes to become a skilled practitioner in this field. And it's really simple when we can improve our life because of this!

As previously discussed in the chapters, learning from everyone who motivates us and has already attained success, including the kind of success we just dream of, is highly beneficial. Everyone can discover their learning method as long as it satisfies their needs and, most importantly, works. Since everyone has various preferences—some people are kinesthetic, others are visual, and others are listeners—it is important to select the one that will help you get the most out of the time you spend learning neuro-linguistic programming.

Neuro-linguistic programming approaches are frequently blended with psychology, counseling, coaching, or education. To become a role model for others who are still searching for their way of life, advice on how to succeed, or just someone to learn useful skills from that will help them not only in their daily lives but also in changing for the better in themselves; it is, therefore, worthwhile to broaden your horizons and become one of those people who have achieved the successes they have always dreamed of. Now is the time to start expanding your understanding of NLP!

Brian Tracy is another fascinating and motivating individual. He is a well-known motivational speaker, and if you're searching for fresh approaches to reaching your objectives, he will undoubtedly serve as a fantastic inspiration. You will understand the value of self-control and become more effective in your actions as a result of it. There is something for everyone in his array of training packages, which are offered as audiobooks and videos. The author's publications, "Change Your Thinking, Change Your Life," as well as many more publications of this author.

To be as productive as possible, each person must discover the approach that works for them; regarding Brian Tracy, a large portion of his writings and talkscenter on the psychology of success and personal growth. Like Tony Robbins, he is a well-known author with a global following and best-selling books. Tracy is a great resource for learning about business, leadership, efficient sales techniques, time management, and self-control. Examining the resumes of people like Anthony Robbins and Brian Tracy is also highly motivating because it shows that you can achieve greatness and inspire people worldwide if you are driven, diligent, and willing to learn and grow.

Begin your adventure now, where you will overcome your obstacles. Resolve your issues and become an aspirant individual aware of your goals and desires. No matter what circumstances we find ourselves in, there is always a chance for success. The best course of action is to solve problems, make goals for the future, and follow through on them. Because among close friends, what could be greater than the realization of the deepest desires? Take off on the journey of a lifetime and begin pursuing your dreams right away! Spend no time in standing still. Everyone has the potential to grow in their abilities and, most importantly, to transform. When properly executed, this investment cannot be used against us and can potentially improve our lives. Decide that you will make a change for the better in your relationships, set goals, and begin to grow. Because your choice will fundamentally alter who you are as a person.

Second tip: What matters to you?

What matters to you personally? Which is it—your passion, your job, your family, or your career? Generally, our values in life have an impact on our decisions. For example, if you value your family highly, you probably want to ensure that each member is content, healthy, and able to fulfill their desires. If you value your career highly, you'll constantly seek methods to advance in that field. Because of this, it is quite simple for someone to take advantage of you if they see a gap in your values. For example, someone can make you an offer that seems like a good fit, like paying for your college education in return for something else.

Make sure that most of your fundamental needs are satisfied to close these gaps. Make no excuses for your failures. Identify strategies for improving your life. Don't give in.

Tip 3: Take independent action.
Nothing is more motivating than implementing the choices you have made for yourself. That is why a manipulator assures you that you do not learn their motives. Most of us place less weight on decisions others make than on our own free will. Personal choices largely determine success. Once you begin to make decisions, manipulators will find it difficult to sway you. You give someone else the power to rule your life

when you let them decide for you. You will be reliant on them and helpless without them forever. Furthermore, it gives you greater confidence to make your own decisions. Every choice you make, win or lose, is a teaching moment.

Tip #4: Assume accountability

Being accountable for your choices and their outcomes is the definition of taking responsibility. People tend to put off making important decisions because they don't want to fail. Because it is our human tendency to find someone to blame when anything goes wrong, most individuals hesitate to make important decisions out of fear of what might happen.

In most situations, our insecurity prevents us from making important judgments. You must have a set of principles and beliefs that serve as a life framework to alleviate these worries. Consequently, your decision-making process will be easy. Many factors come into play when you accept responsibility for your choices.

- You get empowerment first. Each wise choice you make boosts your self-assurance.

Secondly, you will never be a victim if things do not turn out as you hoped. You are not a victim of the poor judgments made by others because you made that decision based solely on your judgment.

Thirdly, you have the freedom to alter your opinion at any moment. Changing your mind midway through someone else's plan might be very difficult.

Fourthly, making wise decisions helps you to be ready for any eventuality. You can examine every possible result while you analyze your options.

- Lastly, if you begin to make your own decisions, you will get the respect of others. A manipulator won't have the chance to dictate your decisions.

Recognize That Not Every Choice You Make Will Work Out Well For You.

A fear of the result prevents most of us from making decisions. Some of us even want to know the outcome before the procedure begins. One cannot make decisions because of this dread, especially if they are essential. Prioritizing results over other considerations impedes our decision-making ability and leads to counterproductive behavior.

Today's world is incredibly chaotic, with unexpected events occurring almost every other minute. As a result, it is exceedingly difficult to accurately forecast the outcomes of our choices.

Because life is moving quickly, you must make some decisions before things become even more hectic. Recognize that you are not required to be aware of the outcome. Additionally, be aware that nothing will improve if you don't decide. All you can do is figure out what to do immediately. In this manner, you will progressively approach your goal. The nicest thing is that, although it's not always possible, you can alter your mind anytime.

Making decisions gets easier the more you do it and understand how to avoid manipulation.

Tip 6: Examine and amend

Evaluating the legitimacy of any decision-making process or method after it has been identified is critical. To what extent has the process enhanced your life, and are there any actions you may take to improve it? Are you making progress toward your goals? If there are any gaps, try to find a means to close them. It's fascinating to note that change is the only constant in life, even though sometimes people feel compelled to follow plans once they are formed. Don't hesitate to adjust your process if something is not working for you.

Tip 7: Allowance for modification
Always give yourself wiggle room. Permitting oneself to change plans to

suit your preferences. In this manner, you'll be aware of what's happening both within and outside of you, making it easier to recognize a manipulator when one comes along. The secret to learning new things is change.

Tip 8: Resist the need to modify

This tip is valid even though it contradicts the preceding one, which could make it sound confusing. In essence, following a plan could enable you to accomplish your objective. Adhere to your decision for as long as possible before making a change. Most prosperous people will tell you that maintaining consistency is essential.

Don't let obstacles cause you to second-guess yourself every time. Never give up on a task just because you encounter difficulty. Sometimes, you just need to persevere for a little while longer. Therefore, make your own decisions unless it is evident that the objective you have set for yourself is no longer achievable. If you have to adjust, make sure you fully commit to the new path.

Decision-making skills and avoid manipulators and those who influence others' minds.

How Do You Perform Hypnosis?

Scientists are not precisely sure how or why hypnotism works, as they are with many other brain phenomena, but thanks to recent EEG scans of the hypnotic brain, they are getting closer to the solution. Dr. Mark Jensen discovered that the neurophysiological properties of hypnosis and meditation are comparable.

"In both cases, the slow-wave brain activity that occurs during relaxation and concentration will increase, while the fast-wave brain activity related to thinking and processing will decrease," Jensen said in an interview with The Little Mystery of Life.

When treating chronic pain, Jensen examines the patient's brain while prescribing hypnotics. "All pain is managed in the brain," he said. "It is first registered in the sensory cortex, but the frontal cortex interprets it, and the thalamus or other regions experience anxiety and tension due to pain.

"You can ask individuals to envision the sensation that normally does not occur during hypnosis since severe pain is usually modest and does not create distress. The frontal brain and other areas will start to become less active right away. Put another way, patients are altering how their brains interpret pain."

During hypnosis, almost 80% of Jensen patients report significant pain alleviation; for 50%, the decline lasts for many hours. Many patients have learned to treat their pain automatically by self-medicating.

Applications of Hypnosis

The ASCH states that hypnosis has been in some form or another for as long as records are recorded. The history of modern clinical hypnosis dates back to the late 1700s, and it has been a generally accepted type of therapy since 1958.

You Could Experience the Traumatic Event Again

Depending on what you see as a hypnotherapist, you may want to prepare for unpleasant memories and emotional shocks. As Gitch puts it: "Some hypnotherapists are trained in illegal deflation. These deflations are achieved through the experience of suppressing emotions, expression, and subsequent release of suppressed emotions."

Let's say you wish to forgive someone who has wronged you while you are hypnotized. It may not be comfortable at first, but this is all part of the process, according to Gucci, who stated: "In forgiveness work, clients have been instructed to become 'criminals.'" "Clients feel uneasy when they face changes in the person who hurt them."

Our automatic, unconscious thoughts cause stereotypes," hypnotherapist Grace Smith told Bustle. "Smokers experience it." "Automatic craving, which triggers the conscious mind to smoke."

Treatment is the answer to all of these. However, this is advantageous. According to Smith: "Smokers can reconstruct these unconscious impulses through hypnosis. Initially, they will investigate the source of these automatic ideas.

Hypnosis can assist in identifying the underlying cause of habit or stubbornness. "After that, smokers can begin to delete, update, or replace more thoughts. Positive thoughts are pushed to the forefront of the unconscious, overwhelming old ways of thinking."

It's Possible to Reprogram

CPC's thought process is divided into three parts, according to clinical hypnotherapist Traci Blank, FIBH, CMS-

CHt: conscious, subconscious, and superconscious. The "key factor" lies between the subconscious and the superconscious.

"During the hypnosis process, we open up the key element of entering the subconscious," Blank stated. "So, hypnotherapy is just a process through which we can access the subconscious mind to discover the beliefs of existence and change the program to meet your goals better. I always tell my clients that it knows how the mind works. Yes, and then use that knowledge to make it a reality. Work for you."

It Must Work for You.

In the same way, their will cannot hypnotize anyone. Reprogramming time and these solutions are only effective when someone needs them. "Everyone can enter hypnosis, but three things must be done: desire, you must enter a hypnotic state; faith, you must believe that you can enter a hypnotic state; safety, you must be able to be in your environment and feel safe when leading you with you." "When all these things are ready, hypnosis will happen."

It is well worth your time to give hypnotherapy a try. An open mind will help, even though nobody anticipates being "cured" during treatment.

Unhealthy Connections and Friendships

Things become more difficult when it comes to handling manipulative friends and family. Most individuals frequently find it difficult to recognize manipulation when a close friend or relative is involved. This is a result of our loved ones blindsiding us with their affection. When someone is your love, you don't think they could harm you. Most of the time, we remain guarded even if an outsider notices we are being manipulated. You must maintain sobriety and consider every one of your interactions carefully. You need to assess the individuals in your life to see if they are manipulating you. Recognize the warning signals of manipulation, which might originate from anyone in your immediate vicinity.

Indices That Your Friend or Partner Is Cheating on You

Using your affection to get favors: If someone close to you is always taking advantage of your enthusiasm to get blessings, there's a good possibility that you are being manipulated. Steer clear of those who ask questions like "If you love," "Do you care about me?" and similar ones. Usually, people make these kinds of statements to force someone to do something they do not want to.

Playing mind games: Someone close to you is likely attempting to take control of your life if they consistently play mind games with you. Examples of mind games are when someone plays the hard-to-get and makes you feel guilty. Someone could act needy to obtain your favor. Any members of your immediate family who might try to manipulate you mentally into changing who you are need to be watched closely.

They are projecting: Projecting is one of the most widely used techniques of relationship manipulation. Your partner is likely attempting to take control of your life if you see that they are constantly transferring their mistakes onto you.

Deception: Lying indicates that someone is attempting to control your life. Steer clear of those always spreading lies about you and your life. A manipulative individual will stop at nothing to obtain the desired outcome in a relationship.

Handling It and Making It Right

We are the ones who have solutions for every toxic relationship, even though we let harmful individuals into our lives. The length of time you have been together is irrelevant. You have to be able to handle any poisonous relationship and come up with a long-term fix. In a toxic relationship, you will come out on the short end of the stick. Even though the connection could appear significant at first, you will ultimately suffer a loss in your life. So, what is the actual protocol for handling toxic friends and family members?

Face them: You must confront the person causing the negative in your life if you have discovered who they are. You have to confront someone if they undermine your self-worth or attempt to control you and take advantage of your resources.

Cut them off: In some situations, you just have to give up on giving the manipulator the things that keep them around. Children frequently use their parents' affection as leverage and manipulate them into giving them money.

Cut off all communication: When handling manipulative people, cutting off all communication is an alternative. If you give a manipulative person access to your life, they will come to you more often. But they have to cease if you close off all avenues of communication via which they can enter your life. If you engage in any social or familial interaction with a manipulative individual, manipulation will begin to spread.

Relationships That Are Toxic and What to Do About Them

Relationships with toxic people are common. They might manifest as openly harmful interpersonal interactions or as subtly destructive ones. Toxic relationships can erode someone's confidence and peace of mind, regardless of the true nature of the connection. For this reason, we'll discuss what constitutes a toxic relationship, its different kinds, and ways to avoid it. Any type of relationship that hurts at least one of the parties involved can be broadly classified as toxic. Making this distinction is crucial since some toxic relationships harm all parties involved or just one of the parties (there must be two persons engaged). There may be emotional, physical, or both types of injury in this kind of relationship. One kind of injury is typically more common than the other. Sometimes, both might be present at the same time. Nevertheless, a toxic relationship will hurt the people in it in a way that can have long-lasting consequences. Think about this instance:

One partner in a marriage abuses the other physically. Usually, the victim endures the abuse for a variety of reasons. Let's argue that the victim stays in the relationship despite feeling afraid. As a result, the victimizer seizes the opportunity to further subjugate their victim. Ultimately, the victim's physical suffering could result in fatalities or other severe physical injuries. In this instance, most of the harm is caused to one of the parties because they receive the abuse. The victimizer's actions could cause them to experience mental discomfort. For example, although this is not always the case, the victimizer could experience guilt after abusing their spouse. Let's examine a scenario where both partners experience harm from their poisonous relationship. This scenario involves mental harm rather than physical harm to any spouse. There is verbal abuse between the two spouses. They often get into yelling battles where they say many hurtful things to each other. The outcome is more emotional agony than either partner has ever known. Both sides in this situation have two roles—victim and victimizer. This inevitably results in a relationship collapse, which is typically irreversible. This implies that the abuse will keep happening until the relationship dissolves. Nonetheless, both partners may be so committed to one another that it seems unthinkable to them to end the relationship. A cycle of maltreatment that continues for years on end could be the outcome.

When and where else are hypnotic language patterns applicable?

This tactic works well in sales situations and interpersonal interactions with friends, family, and coworkers. People vary; thus, even if hypnotic language patterns have been tried and tested numerous times, there is always a degree of unpredictability. But regardless of the situation, applying this tactic will undoubtedly result in a better, more favorable response to recommendations.

Last Goal:

In conclusion, it's important to remember that the seller ultimately makes a product or service sell, regardless of how intricately crafted it may be. He is responsible for ensuring a customer is persuaded to buy whatever is being offered. The sales representative's skill set is more important than the product's functionality. This is where hypnotic language patterns might be useful, serving two purposes: first, to facilitate transactions, and second, to increase the productivity of sellers. A product cannot, after all, sell itself!

Using Meta-Models: A Guide

Finding the violations is a necessary first step in applying meta-models. This procedure is described as follows:

First, find instances of meta-model violations.

This is the first step in admitting you made a mistake.

Step 2: Ask Yourself Questions: Asking yourself questions will help you find out the truth when you suspect a violation.

Step 3: Test: Determine ways to prevent making the same error twice.

Can Meta-Models be applied elsewhere?

Meta models have applications in nearly every aspect of life. Meta-models can be very helpful in personal and professional interactions because they make it possible to communicate any message efficiently.

Last Goal:

Knowing meta-models is essential to improving as a sales professional. They improve the capacity for straightforward communication, which draws and holds the customer's interest. In summary, these meta-models foster the seller's overall growth, increase confidence, and foster positive customer relations. This will guarantee that the expert nearly always converts "prospective" clients into "definite" customers.

Creating A Viable New Belief

Make sure the new belief fits the person you want to become before attempting to shift your beliefs. At this point, you must be honest with yourself because decisions made while under misconception seldom last. Part of the process of committing to a change is also understanding why you are doing it. An ecological check is the process of making sure the new belief aligns with your values.

The environment check may be completed quickly or require some time to complete. It could be easy to adopt a new belief and take a little work to incorporate it into your life. But you might also need to do some fact-checking. You might have a few queries for yourself. Does this suit my emotional personality? What does this new belief hold for me? Does the influence of this new belief make me want to stick with it and resist the want to go back to my old belief? Do these values align with mine? How much would this modification cost, and am I willing to pay it?

Think of this ecological assessment as your due diligence before completely changing your perspective on life. It's a means to make sure there are no reasons for the commitment to back down after you make it and to check your intentions for any leaks. Now that you've completed your research, the only possible consequence is that you will succeed in implementing your new belief.

V - Pacing in the Future

Achieving our objectives and setting them are two very different things, and part of the difficulty is in preparing ourselves for the journey there. Being ready to be the kind of person ready to accomplish the objectives we set for ourselves is another aspect of the task. According to most successful people, seeing yourself evolve along the way is one of the most fulfilling aspects of pursuing your goals. It makes sense to focus a lot of energy on getting ready for that shift and feeling ready to act when it comes.

When we make big, bold goals, we often underestimate their difficulty. It's easy to become engrossed in picturing a bad experience:

It will be difficult to write that paper.

It seems impossible to work out consistently for six months.

I'm going to lose it over this project's timeline.

It's also simple to forget to be explicit about those difficulties and practice mentally conquering them. We frequently neglect to prepare for unknowns that may arise along the route. But just as a competitor practices a strategy thousands of times before a big game, we can use neurolinguistic programming to set ourselves up for success as we go toward our greatest goals.

Numerous studies have repeatedly demonstrated that when an athlete watches another athlete execute an action, their muscles fire with the same electrical impulses as if they were doing the exercise themselves. Athletes who see themselves doing the maneuver also feel the actual impulses. Do you recall mirror neurons? Indeed, they are in play here, and we have the power to utilize them to our benefit. We can picture our best performance to increase our chances of success, much like athletes do.

First and foremost, we must cultivate the idea that our journey will be enjoyable. Combining several approaches yields more potent outcomes.

The aim is to set expectations for success, contentment, and enjoyment in whatever path we take, regardless of the approach. Emotions and language are important tools that we must carefully use to our benefit. For instance, we must employ strong tools like "easily" and "comfortably" when writing affirmations. These words emphasize positive experiences. This quarter, I will comfortably reach the top 10% of my company's global stack rankings. In the following three months, I will shed ten pounds.

It makes all the difference in the world to start with the destination in mind and assume that the journey will be positive to cultivate a mindset that is ready to endure. When imagining success, place a heavy emphasis on emotions of fulfillment, accomplishment, and enjoyment. Allow these emotions to serve as your beacon of hope as you continue on your journey.

While this initial step is crucial for laying the groundwork for success, we still need to figure out how. A difficult and turbulent road leads from Point A to Point B. Just like an athlete practices drills to help compete against highly talented opponents, these are nothing to be alarmed about or a threat to our success if we are adequately prepared for them. But if you don't prepare for and practice these obstacles, it's as though you're the only one applying for a promotion. It's like preparing to be the only team playing football. You are positioning yourself for failure.

When people give up while pursuing their objectives, it's usually because they weren't well-prepared for the journey. When presented with his first large task, a student may feel overwhelmed by increasing responsibilities and nearly fail, even with the greatest intentions to earn a 4.0 GPA. Why? Because he didn't practice for the sixteen weeks of daily classes, leading study groups, and staying up late writing papers—he practiced simply for the number on his transcript. The obstacles were unexpected, and he was ill-prepared to face them.

On the other hand, a manager getting ready for a C-suite interview could begin by picturing herself at her new corner office, with its maple-stained desk. She's also estimated the number of rehearsal hours she'll need to put in over the following month to prepare for the Board. She's imagined her heart pounding hard as she settles into the interview chair. She's imagined the serenity that comes over her as soon as she greets and gets comfortable with the interviewers. She imagined being asked a question she wasn't ready for by the interviewers, that she would coolly accept their probing to gain some time to gather her thoughts, and that she would craft a compelling response. She had envisioned the anxious days after the interview when she got signs of self-doubt and anxiety. She has also imagined the scene: Tuesday morning, she opens her email to find an offer letter from the Chairman herself.

These two people prepared very differently to achieve their lofty final objectives. The student did not prepare for the procedure or the inevitable obstacles that would arise, and he was unprepared to deal with them when they did. However, the manager had already imagined her nervousness before even walking into the meeting and the moment when she was asked a question for which she was unprepared. There was no uncertainty or concern when those things occurred. Since she had imagined herself there, she felt equipped to deal with it.

Our mirror neurons provide us with an effective tool to practice for difficult situations and benefit from neurolinguistic programming. We can often predict with some degree of accuracy what will happen along the route, and we can prepare to the point where we are equipped to deal with such events. Most crucially, we may picture ourselves in the right frame of mind at the precise moment when we need it. And we can get ready for such specific times because of NLP and our imagination.

www.ingramcontent.com/pod-product-compliance
Lightning Source LLC
Chambersburg PA
CBHW052146110526
44591CB00012B/1882